FACTS ABOUT THE CASSOWARY

By Lisa Strattin

© 2020 Lisa Strattin

FREE BOOK

FREE FOR ALL SUBSCRIBERS

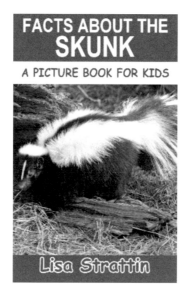

LisaStrattin.com/Subscribe-Here

BOX SET

- **FACTS ABOUT THE POISON DART FROGS**
- **FACTS ABOUT THE THREE TOED SLOTH**
  - **FACTS ABOUT THE RED PANDA**
  - **FACTS ABOUT THE SEAHORSE**
  - **FACTS ABOUT THE PLATYPUS**
  - **FACTS ABOUT THE REINDEER**
  - **FACTS ABOUT THE PANTHER**
- **FACTS ABOUT THE SIBERIAN HUSKY**

LisaStrattin.com/BookBundle

Facts for Kids Picture Books by Lisa Strattin

Little Blue Penguin, Vol 92

Chipmunk, Vol 5

Frilled Lizard, Vol 39

Blue and Gold Macaw, Vol 13

Poison Dart Frogs, Vol 50

Blue Tarantula, Vol 115

African Elephants, Vol 8

Amur Leopard, Vol 89

Sabre Tooth Tiger, Vol 167

Baboon, Vol 174

Sign Up for New Release Emails Here

http://LisaStrattin.com/subscribe-here

Contents

INTRODUCTION

The cassowary is a large bird, believed to be a remnant of the dinosaurs. It is similar to the ostrich and the emu, but is generally smaller than either. They are flightless birds, just like the emu and ostrich. There are three species of cassowary, with distinct characteristics and domiciles, but all are found in New Guinea, Australia and the surrounding islands.

CHARACTERISTICS

The southern cassowary is usually found in New Guinea and Australia and is the largest of the three species. The dwarf is typically found in the higher elevations of New Guinea and the island of New Britain. The northern cassowary lives in New Guinea's northern lowlands. The bird is shy and generally not seen by humans as it will usually retreat to the dense rain forest when approached.

They are heavier than the emu, although they are shorter. The only bird larger in weight and height is the ostrich.

They are more active at dusk and dawn, making them crepuscular), but they are difficult to observe in the wild because they hide in the rain forest.

They have a four inch claw on the inner toe of each foot and are considered very dangerous. They have been known to kill humans with the deadly claws. They kick and use the claws like a knife against any threat. They can run up to 31 miles per hour or 50 kilometers, even through thick underbrush.

The cassowary can jump to a height of seven feet (2 meters). The cassowary is also an accomplished swimmer.

The cassowary communicates by hissing and whistling and have also been known to rumble or growl. They will also clap their bills to communicate.

APPEARANCE

Each species of cassowary has a casque or helmet. The casque is made of material similar to human fingernails. The females have larger casques than the males, but no one really knows the purpose of the casque. It is believed that the casques amplify the sounds the cassowary makes or provide protection for the skull when the birds run through the rain forest.

The bird is covered with long two-quilled feathers that can look like hair and they are almost always black as adults. The feathers act as protection and keep the birds dry in the rain forest.

Bare quills hang from the small wings of the cassowary and the wings are not large enough or strong enough to enable the bird to fly.

Unlike other types of birds, the female cassowary is more brightly colored than the males. The heads are bright blue. The northern cassowary has one brightly colored wattle while the southern cassowary has two. The wattles are patches of skin that hang from the neck. They are blue, red, gold, purple or white depending on the species. No one knows what purpose the wattles serve, but it is believed they reflect the mood of the bird or provide social cues to other cassowaries. Since the bird is so shy and has not been adequately studied in the wild, it is only a guess.

The dwarf cassowary does not have a wattle, but instead has a bright purple spot where the wattle would be. It also has bright pink spots on the cheeks.

LIFE STAGES

Cassowaries live alone except for when mating or caring for the young. Breeding is from June to October each year. When paired off for mating, the pair will stay together for a few weeks, building the nest, until the female is ready to lay eggs.

The females, after mating, will lay three to five eggs (a clutch) that are each about five inches long and weigh about one and a half pounds. The male then incubates the eggs for about fifty days in a nest made of leaves and located on the ground and will care for the hatchlings. The female may mate again with another male and lay another clutch of eggs in another nest and that male will incubate those eggs.

The chicks are brown and tan striped. The male teaches the chicks to feed and they stay with the male for anyway from nine to sixteen months. The male with then run them off and look for a new female to breed again. By the time the chicks leave, they are almost the size of an adult cassowary.

LIFE SPAN

The cassowary reaches maturity at two and a half to three years of age. In the wild, the cassowary usually lives about 19 years. They have lived for 40 years in zoos.

SIZE

The southern cassowary is the largest of the species, at about five feet (1.5 meters) tall. Some females can be six and half feet tall and weigh as much as 130 pounds (58.5 kg). Females are larger than the males.

The dwarf cassowary is about three to three and a half feet tall and weighs about 63 pounds (29 kg).

HABITAT

Cassowaries live in the rainforests and wetlands of New Guinea, northern Australia and the surrounding islands. Although they are not on any endangered list, they are in danger of losing their habitat to humans – much of the rainforest of northern Australia has been cleared.

Cassowaries will stay in a particular "home" area and will defend the area against intruders.

DIET

The diet of the adult cassowaries consists of fruits, flowers, snails, insects, fish, frogs, birds, mice and rats. They will eat the whole fruit when the fruit drops from the trees. The diet is comprised predominantly of fruit, with the fruit of the laurel, podocarp, palm, wild grape, nightshade and myrtle trees/bushes being of particular importance to the cassowary. They are frugivorous but are also considered omnivorous.

FRIENDS AND ENEMIES

The cassowary can fall prey to wild hogs, crocodiles, wild dogs and humans. They have no friends and tend to be solitary with the females defending their home area much more fiercely than the males.

SUITABILITY AS PETS

They are too shy and too dangerous to be kept as pets. They have not been bred successfully in zoos and it is very difficult and costly to recreate the necessary habitat to keep a cassowary as a pet. In addition, their large size would make it impractical. However, some societies in New Guinea have been known to capture the chicks and raise them. They remain only semi-tame and can be extremely dangerous to humans and domestic animals.

COLOR ME

COLOR ME

COLOR ME

COLOR ME

COLOR ME

COLOR ME

COLOR ME

COLOR ME

COLOR ME

Please leave me a review here:

http://lisastrattin.com/Review-Vol-388

For more Kindle Downloads Visit Lisa Strattin Author Page on Amazon Author Central

http://amazon.com/author/lisastrattin

To see upcoming titles, visit my website at LisaStrattin.com– all books available on kindle!

http://lisastrattin.com

FREE BOOK

FOR ALL SUBSCRIBERS – SIGN UP NOW

LisaStrattin.com/Subscribe-Here

Lisa Strattin.com/Facebook

LisaStrattin.com/Youtube

Made in the USA
Columbia, SC
20 December 2024

50343694R00024